A DAY IN THE LIFE OF A
Rock Musician

by David Paige

photography by Roger Ruhlin

Troll Associates

Library of Congress Catalog Card Number: 78-68808
ISBN 0-89375-225-8   ISBN 0-89375-229-0 Paper Edition

The author and publisher wish to thank Audiotronix Sound Studios, Hedden West Sound Studios, Rich Moyers,
Stephen Titra, Ellen Titra, and Jim Seyller for their generous assistance and cooperation.

Last night, Rich Moyers got to bed at three o'clock in the morning. That's not unusual for him. Rich is a rock musician, and he often performs late at night. Then he sleeps until noon, gets up, and has a cup of coffee at his piano. Although Rich plays guitar with his group, he composes his music on the piano.

Rich writes both words and music for his songs. And he has already recorded some of the songs for his first album. Today, he wants to work on a new song before he leaves for rehearsal. So Rich is up at ten o'clock. That's early for him.

After an hour at the piano, there is ordinary business to attend to. He pays some bills. He talks with his agent about holding a concert at a nearby college. He schedules studio time for next week. He calls his record producer to talk about the songs his group will record today.

In the early afternoon, he and the rest of his group prepare to go to the rehearsal studio. If the group were well known, they would have other people, called "roadies," to carry their equipment around and set it up. But they are not well known yet, so they do their own loading and unloading.

Rich performs with an electric guitar. He has several different guitars, and each one is worth between $500 and $1000. At this rehearsal, he will be playing an electric six-string guitar. Tonight, at a live performance, he will use his twelve-string guitar.

Ellen is the group's keyboardist. She plays keyboard instruments such as the piano, organ, and synthesizer. When she appears with Rich Moyers' group, she plays rock music. In her own solo appearances, she plays classical music. Ellen is the only member of the group who doesn't have to lug her instrument from studio to studio.

The drummer, Jim, has the biggest job of packing and unpacking. Each drum, cymbal, supporting rod, and foot pedal is packed separately. Jim also plays the congo drum, tambourines, maracas, and wind chimes — when the musical arrangement calls for them.

Steve plays bass guitar with the group, but he can also play other kinds of guitars. Like any other guitar, his four-string electric bass has to be tuned each time he uses it. The bass guitar and drums provide the rhythm, while the melody is played on the lead guitar.

The group will be rehearsing a new piece of music that Rich has written for the album. Ellen studies the sheet music, and comes up with something slightly different for the piano part. She talks to Rich about it.

Rehearsing is much more than a matter of sitting down and playing a song again and again. The musicians must go over the music together, discuss their individual parts, and decide how each person will play. Then they can experiment until everything sounds just the way they want it to.

A single song may be rehearsed as many as fifty times before everything is just right. That's why rehearsals are held in small studios, where rental costs are low, or in empty lofts or warehouses, where the space is free. But the actual recording will be done in a large studio, where a few hours can be very costly.

At the end of a three-hour rehearsal, Rich meets with the designer who is working on the album cover. Rich approves the cover idea. The designer tells him that a photographer will shoot the cover photograph tonight, at the restaurant where Rich's group is performing.

When Rich and the group arrive at the recording studio, the sound engineer introduces himself. A good recording studio like this one is soundproofed from floor to ceiling. Carpeting and heavy drapes eliminate echoes, so the microphones can pick up each note exactly as it is played.

Mark, the sound engineer, will run the recording session. He is the technician who controls the volume and tone quality of each instrument and the vocal portion of the recording. He discusses the music with Rich as the rest of the group sets up.

Mark has been a sound engineer for more than five years. He knows just where to place a microphone so it will pick up the right amount of sound from the drums and the piano. The electric guitars send their sound directly through the control board to the tape machines, so they do not need microphones.

At the control panel, Mark is ready to begin the recording session. The songs will be recorded on a 16-track tape. Each instrument is recorded on a separate track, and so is Rich's singing. Each track is controlled by the sound engineer. With so many tracks on the tape, the group can decide to fix something later, and it can be electronically added into the recording.

During the actual recording, the group plays together just as it rehearsed. To record one three-minute song may take well over an hour — with 15 or 20 "run-throughs," as they're called. At this session Rich and his group hope to record two songs for the album. Other songs will be recorded at other sessions.

The two songs are recorded in two hours. Then the group takes a well-earned break, and chats about what's happening in the entertainment industry. Meanwhile, the sound engineer edits the recording. The tracks will then be "mixed," or combined into one master tape.

Rich joins Mark and the producer in the control room. They listen as the different tracks are being mixed. The sound engineer pushes the buttons to get different tones and volumes, but it is Rich and the producer who tell him just what they want. And when the job is done, they like what they've got.

Finally, when most people are on their way home from work, the group is off for lunch and an hour's relaxation. Before long, they will have to change their clothes and get ready for the performance they are scheduled to put on this evening.

Tonight they are appearing at a restaurant that offers entertainment as well as dinner. Rich and his group are usually booked for at least ten engagements every month. They play at coffeehouses, nightclubs, school dances, and sometimes at rock concerts.

Dressing rooms are not always available everywhere the group entertains. But the members of the group always find some place to get themselves ready. They know that how they look is an important part of their image.

Once Rich has changed, he comes out and tests the mike. Sound is just as important in a performance as it is in a recording session. Now is the time to take care of technical and mechanical problems — not when the audience is there, waiting to be entertained.

Lighting is the responsibility of the electrician. He dims the lights when they should be dimmed, and brightens them when they should be brightened. And he sets the spotlight. Rich shows the electrician where he is going to stand when he is playing.

The group has rehearsed the songs they are to play, and they have played them before in public. But like even the most experienced performers, they are nervous before the show. A little joking helps to ease the tension before the audience arrives.

At nine o'clock, lights brighten the stage. The performance gets under way and the performers forget their nervousness. They are professional musicians. They know their instruments. They know their music. They concentrate completely on their work.

Solos can be the most difficult. Rich is out there all alone. All eyes and ears are on him. This is where long hours of rehearsals pay off. For as soon as he gets into a song, he feels right at home in the spotlight. There's nothing quite like performing before a live audience.

Later, while the members of the group take a break, a photographer gets ready to take some pictures for the cover of the Rich Moyers album. He uses a light meter to get the right exposure. When the film has been processed, the designer will choose the best of several shots, and use it to complete his cover design.

The talents and efforts of many people are required to produce an album. The performance is, of course, most important. But there is also the sound engineering, the mixing of all the individual tracks into one record, the actual pressing of the record, and the creation of an album cover. Being good enough to cut an album is an exciting achievement for a rock musician.

At two o'clock in the morning, the performance is over. The other members of the group have packed up and gone home. Now Rich Moyers is going home, too. It's the end of another exciting day in the life of a rock musician.